11/16

# WETLAND
# ECOSYSTEMS

by Nikole Brooks Bethea

Content Consultant
Rod Chimner
Associate Professor of Wetland Ecology
Michigan Technological University

Core Library

An Imprint of Abdo Publishing
abdopublishing.com

**abdopublishing.com**

Published by Abdo Publishing, a division of ABDO, PO Box 398166, Minneapolis, Minnesota 55439. Copyright © 2016 by Abdo Consulting Group, Inc. International copyrights reserved in all countries. No part of this book may be reproduced in any form without written permission from the publisher. Core Library™ is a trademark and logo of Abdo Publishing.

Printed in the United States of America, North Mankato, Minnesota
032015
092015

Cover Photo: iStockphoto
Interior Photos: iStockphoto, 1, 4, 6, 8, 10, 13, 16, 22, 28 (top), 28 (top left), 28 (bottom), 28 (bottom left), 28 (bottom right), 30, 36; Shutterstock Images, 18, 20, 24, 26, 28 (top right), 28 (middle), 28 (middle right), 43, 45; Dezidor CC 3.0, 28 (middle left); Jemeema Carrigan/University of Florida/AP Images, 33; Steve Jessmore/The Sun News/AP Images, 34; Edwin Remsberg/VWPics/Newscom, 38

Editor: Jon Westmark
Series Designer: Becky Daum

**Library of Congress Control Number: 2015931588**

**Cataloging-in-Publication Data**
Bethea, Nikole Brooks.
 Wetland ecosystems / Nikole Brooks Bethea.
   p. cm. -- (Ecosystems of the world)
Includes bibliographical references and index.
ISBN 978-1-62403-858-7
1. Wetland ecology--Juvenile literature. 2. Wetlands--Juvenile literature.
I. Title.
577.68--dc23

                                              2015931588

# CONTENTS

# WHAT IS A WETLAND?

**A**n American alligator creeps into the brown waters of the Okefenokee Swamp. Its strong tail sweeps back and forth. The alligator swims just below the water's surface. Only its raised nostrils and eyes are visible as it glides through floating lily pads. Bald cypress trees grow in the water near the shoreline. A sandhill crane wades between the trees' swollen trunks. Its bugle-like call drowns out the

American alligators live only in wetlands of the southeastern United States.

In some wetlands, such as the Okefenokee Swamp, water covers most of the ground year-round.

croaking of the tree frogs. A turtle sunning on a log dives into the dark water with a splash.

## Properties of a Wetland

Water is present in all ecosystems. But it plays a unique role in wetland ecosystems. Swamps, such as the Okefenokee, are one type of wetland. Marshes, bogs, and fens are also types of wetlands. So what makes a wet area a wetland? All wetlands share similar water, soil, and plant characteristics.

Wetlands have hydric soils. This means the soil does not get much oxygen because there is too

### Okefenokee Swamp

The Okefenokee Swamp is one of the largest freshwater swamps in the world. It covers 438,000 acres (177,000 ha) of land in southeast Georgia and northwest Florida. The swamp's name comes from the Creek tribe of Native Americans. It means "land of the trembling earth." This is because walking on the swamp's soft ground often causes nearby bushes and shrubs to shake. The waters of the Okefenokee Swamp are brown. The color comes from tannic acid that is released as plants decay.

7

Many species of duck depend on wetlands to nest, find food, and migrate.

much water. Without much oxygen, dead plant material decays very slowly. So wetland soils contain large amounts of partially decayed plant matter. This collects over thousands of years. Wetland soils sometimes smell like rotten eggs. The smell comes from a gas that is produced by bacteria in the plant-rich soil.

Wetland plants are called hydrophytes. These water-loving plants have adapted to grow with little or no oxygen from the soil.

Approximately 5,000 different wetland plants grow in the United States. Many birds, fish, amphibians, reptiles, and mammals also live in wetlands. Humans rely on wetlands to store and clean water. Wetlands are unique ecosystems that need protecting.

## EXPLORE ONLINE

Chapter One discusses what wetlands are and how to identify them. The website below also discusses the definition of wetlands. As you know, every source is different. How is the information on the website different from the information in this chapter? Which information is the same? How do the two sources present information differently? What can you learn from this website?

### Identifying Wetlands
mycorelibrary.com/wetland-ecosystems

# CHAPTER TWO

# A WATER-SOAKED WORLD

Wetlands have changing water levels. They rise and fall with seasons, tides, or floods. Water is constantly moving. It goes from the earth to the atmosphere and back again. This is called the water cycle. It is an important part of wetland creation and maintenance.

The sun is the energy source for the water cycle. The sun heats water in oceans, lakes, and wetlands.

Wetlands like the Pantanal in Brazil have standing water for part of the year and dry conditions for the other part.

As water warms, the energy of its molecules increases. The water molecules move faster and gain enough energy to break the bonds holding them together. These water molecules can leave the body of water as gas, or water vapor. This process is called evaporation.

The water vapor rises into the cooler atmosphere. The molecules slow down, and their energy decreases. Bonds form again between water molecules, creating water droplets. The water vapor has condensed. Condensation is the change from water vapor into liquid. It forms clouds and fog.

Precipitation is water that falls from the clouds. It can be in the form of rain, snow, sleet, or hail. Water from precipitation gathers in streams, lakes, oceans, and wetlands. It may also soak into the ground. This is called infiltration. Water that soaks into the ground is stored there. This groundwater can bubble up as a spring, or it may feed a wetland or stream.

As water moves through the soil, it is sucked up by plant roots. The water then moves through the

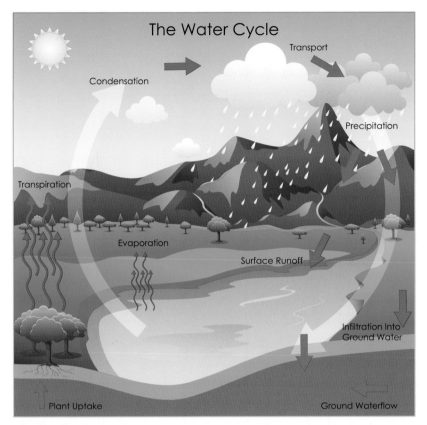

### The Water Cycle Through Wetlands

Wetland water levels are constantly changing because water is always moving. The water cycle is the continuous movement of water on, above, and below the surface of the earth. How does water from a wetland make its way through the water cycle?

plant to pores in the plant's leaves. Next the water heats up and evaporates from the leaves. When leaves release water vapor, it is called transpiration.

# Wetlands and the Water Cycle

The water cycle affects different wetlands in different ways. Some wetlands, such as bogs, depend on rainwater. They are soaked only when there is a lot of precipitation. Other wetlands get water from different places. Some are fed by groundwater, which moves through the soil. Others receive surface water from rivers, lakes, or oceans.

The amount of water in a wetland controls the amount of oxygen in the soil. This determines what plants and animals can live in the wetland.

## Pop-up Wetlands

The Pacific Flyway is a migration route for millions of birds. The path stretches from the Arctic to South America. Birds depend on wetlands in California during their trip. But California has had severe droughts in the past. Conservation groups have worked with California rice farmers to find a solution. The farmers flood their fields in the winter to rot old rice stalks. This creates pop-up wetlands that help the birds survive during droughts.

The following excerpt is from the California Wetlands Information System about management of wetlands in the past:

*Historically, wetland habitat was often seen as only a breeding ground for disease-carrying mosquitos. Federal, State, and local policies to drain, fill, or somehow convert wetlands to more "productive" uses was the norm. For example, the federal Swamp Land Acts of the 1800s gave 65 million acres of wetlands to 15 states, including California, for reclamation. . . . As a result of these and other activities, many of California's wetlands were converted to agricultural and urban uses, and water that had naturally flooded the wetlands was diverted for other needs. Estimates of wetlands that historically existed in California range from 3 to 5 million acres. The current estimate of wetland acreage in California is approximately 450,000 acres; this represents an 85 to 90 percent reduction—the greatest percentage loss in the nation.*

Source: "Past Management Practices." California Wetlands Information System. California Resources Agency, 1998. Web. Accessed February 25, 2015.

## Back It Up

This passage provides evidence to support a point. Write a paragraph describing the claim the passage is making. Write down two or three facts the report uses to support this claim.

# CHAPTER THREE

# WETLAND PLANTS

Wetlands can be grouped into four different types. Each type is based on its location, climate, plants, and soils. The four types of wetlands are marshes, swamps, fens, and bogs.

Marshes are wetlands with soft-stem plants called emergent plants. Their roots are in the soil. But their stems grow above the water. Cattails, bulrushes, arrowheads, and water lilies are a few emergent

Cattails provide habitats for insects, birds, and amphibians.

Bald cypress roots, or knees, extend high out of the ground. They often stick out of the water when the ground is flooded.

plants. Marshes can be freshwater or saltwater. They can be inland or near the coast. Marshes receive most of their water from surface water. But groundwater may also feed marshes.

Woody plants, such as trees and shrubs, grow in swamps. Swamps have standing water for at least part of the year. In forested swamps, trees such as bald cypress and red maple are common. These trees have bases that are buttressed, or flared. This helps anchor the trees into soggy soils. The bald cypress has roots that grow vertically and stick out of the water. These roots are called knees. Scientists believe knees bring oxygen to the trees. Shrub swamps have shrubby plants, such as buttonbush, willow, dogwood, and swamp rose. Forested and shrub swamps may be found beside each other.

## Peatlands

Fens and bogs are also known as peatlands. Peatlands are the most common form of wetland. Grasses, sedges, mosses, and wildflowers often grow in fens. When plants in fens die, they decay very slowly. This creates thick layers of peat. If too much peat builds up, it can cut off the fen's groundwater supply. This can turn the fen into a bog.

## Mangrove Swamps

Mangrove swamps are wetlands found along tropical and subtropical ocean coasts. In the United States, mangrove swamps are found along the Gulf Coast from the tip of Florida to Texas. Salt-tolerant trees and shrubs grow in mangrove swamps. Red mangroves are known for their thick clusters of aboveground, arching roots. Black mangroves have spike-like roots that stick out of the ground. They supply oxygen to the plants growing in the water. Mangroves' root systems protect the coast from erosion during storms.

Sphagnum moss has adapted to live in wet, acidic places.

Bogs receive water and nutrients from precipitation only. This makes them nutrient poor. Sphagnum moss does well in places without a lot of nutrients. It covers the ground like a spongy carpet. Sphagnum moss creates a lot of acid. This limits what other plants and animals can live in bogs. Cranberries and blueberries grow well in bogs. Pitcher plants can also grow in bogs. They get nutrients by trapping and eating insects.

# Changes

Wetlands are always changing. Marshes can turn into swamps as trees grow in them. Swamps can flood and become marshes. Fens can turn into bogs as they form peat.

In all types of wetlands, plants are the primary producers. They use the sun's energy to make their own food. This is called photosynthesis. Plants absorb the sun's energy and use it to change carbon dioxide and water into oxygen and sugar. When an animal eats a wetland plant, the energy transfers from the plant to the animal.

## The Florida Everglades

Humans can also change wetlands. In the Everglades, water once flowed from central Florida south to Lake Okeechobee. From there it moved slowly through saw grass marshes toward the Florida Bay. In some places, the water was only a few inches deep. An Everglades drainage project began in 1905. It turned marshes into farmland. Today people are working to restore the Everglades. It is one of the largest wetland restoration projects in the world.

# CHAPTER FOUR

# WETLAND ANIMALS

Wetlands provide food, shelter, nests, and breeding grounds for animals. In fact more than one-third of the threatened and endangered wildlife in the United States live in wetlands. And approximately half of all threatened and endangered species use wetlands at some time in their lives.

The American crocodile is one wetland species. Habitat loss and illegal hunting have made it an endangered animal.

Beavers dam rivers and streams to create calm ponds and wetlands where they can build their lodges.

## Crucial Habitat

Many types of fish depend on wetlands to survive. Fish use wetlands to find food and breed. Birds also rely on wetlands. Common bird species found here are ducks, geese, and wading birds, such as great blue herons and sandhill cranes. Wetlands provide food and resting places for birds during migration.

A wide variety of mammals use wetlands for food and shelter. Muskrats, minks, beavers, raccoons, and white-tailed deer are common wetland mammals. Some mammals have adaptations to help them live in wetlands. For example, beavers have webbed feet for swimming. They also have large front teeth, called incisors, that allow them to chew through trees on land. They use the trees to build lodges and dams.

Wetlands are home to many amphibians, including spotted salamanders, marbled salamanders,

## Beavers Dams

Beavers build dams to stop flowing water. Water backs up behind dams. If water rises high enough, the stream will flood the surrounding area. This forms a pond. Over time ponds can form wetlands. Creating wetlands is one way beavers live up to their nickname as "nature's engineers." However, beaver dams can be a problem. For instance, a dammed up drainage ditch could wash out a road.

Most reptiles, such as turtles, are cold-blooded. Their body temperature changes with their environment.

gray tree frogs, American toads, and newts. Frogs and salamanders use wetlands for laying eggs. When the eggs hatch, the young animals live in the water. After changing into adults, they spend more time on land.

Many reptiles spend their entire lives in wetlands. They often live near the edge of wetlands where they can use the sun to raise their body temperature. Reptiles use the water to cool themselves. A few wetland reptiles include alligators, common snapping turtles, northern water snakes, and cottonmouth snakes.

## Different Roles

All wetland animals rely on their habitat for food. Some eat plants. These animals are called herbivores. Other animals are carnivores. They only eat other animals. For example, minks prey on frogs and young birds. Animals that eat both plants and animals are called omnivores. Raccoons are a common wetland omnivore. They eat frogs, turtles, seeds, and nuts.

## The American Alligator

Alligators spend their entire lives in wetlands. They have adaptations for living here. Their eyes and nostrils stick up above the water while their bodies hide below the surface. This lets them see and breathe while looking for their next meal. Alligators have an extra pair of eyelids to cover their eyes underwater. These lids act like goggles by helping them to see. Alligators can also close off their nostrils and ears underwater. American alligators became endangered in the 1950s. They were hunted for their skins and meat. By 1987 alligator populations made a full comeback. Alligators were removed from the endangered species list.

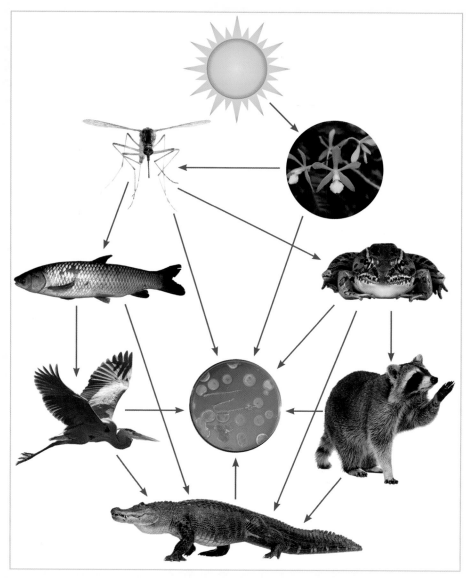

## Wetland Food Web

In this diagram, lines between the organisms show how energy moves through the web. Energy from the sun helps plants grow. Some animals get their energy from plants, while others eat other animals. Bacteria feeds on dead animals and plants. Think of another species you have read about. How might it fit into this food web? How might it connect to other organisms?

The concept of animals depending on plants and other animals for survival is called a food chain. Food chains often overlap because most animals eat more than one type of food. The network of overlapping food chains is called a food web.

In a swamp, an alligator may be at the top of the food chain. It might eat a fish that had eaten a mosquito. The mosquito may have eaten nectar from a flower. Since the flower is a plant, it made its own food using the sun and soil.

Decomposers are at the bottom of the food chain. They get energy by eating dead plants and animals. They also eat waste from other creatures. Decomposers are recyclers. They break down dead plants and animals and return the nutrients to the soil. The nutrients can then help plants grow. Bacteria and fungi are the main decomposers in wetlands.

# CHAPTER FIVE

# PEOPLE AND WETLANDS

**T**here were approximately 221 million acres (89.5 million ha) of wetlands in the United States in the 1600s. But settlers and developers saw wetlands as wastelands because they could not be farmed or used for roads and buildings. People drained and filled in wetlands with soil to make the land more useful. Some wetlands were filled to prevent diseases,

Filling in wetlands changes what soil, plants, and animals can exist there.

## Tampa Bay Wetlands

Northern Tampa Bay, Florida, has more than 33,000 wetlands and many lakes. In the early 2000s, wells pumped about 165 million gallons (625 million L) of groundwater per day. During an ongoing drought, the pumping caused groundwater levels to decrease. Lake levels also dropped, and wetlands dried up. To fix the problem, authorities reduced groundwater pumping. They used more surface water instead. They also removed salt from seawater to get freshwater. These efforts resulted in rising groundwater levels, allowing wetlands to return.

such as malaria. Malaria can spread through mosquitos, which lay their eggs in wetlands. By 2009 only 110 million acres (44.5 million ha) remained.

People have hurt wetlands in other ways too. One way is by introducing invasive species. These species do not live naturally in a certain habitat. They grow rapidly and spread easily in the areas where they are introduced. They overtake native species. For example people have released Burmese pythons into the Everglades. These

Burmese pythons and other invasive species compete with native wildlife and upset the balance of the ecosystem.

large snakes eat native mammals and birds. They even prey on alligators on occasion. Because the pythons have no natural predators, they have a major impact on the ecosystem. Another example of an invasive species common in the Everglades is the melaleuca, also called the paperbark tree. It was introduced to the area in the early 1900s to help dry up the Everglades. Melaleuca has taken over hundreds of thousands of acres of Everglades wetlands. The trees

People can create stormwater wetlands. These help trap and remove pollutants in runoff.

grow up to 80 feet (24 m) tall, keeping the native plants beneath them from getting the sunlight they need to survive.

## Helpful to Humans

Wetlands do many good things for humans. They are natural filters that absorb pollutants from the environment. For example, wetland plants absorb chemicals and nutrients that seep into the water from fertilizers, manure, and septic tanks. Wetlands also help with storm water. As the water slowly moves through wetland plants, particles and soil are filtered out of the water. The water leaves the wetland cleaner than when it entered.

Wetlands can act as sponges to help control flooding. They soak up and store water. This reduces the amount of water that flows down rivers and streams and can help protect homes and property. Stored water is slowly released from the wetland. Much of it seeps into the ground over time. This water can then be pumped to the surface to be used by humans.

## FURTHER EVIDENCE

Chapter Five discusses many functions of wetlands. What is the main point of this chapter? What key evidence supports this point? Go to the article about wetlands at the website below. Find a quote from the website that supports the chapter's main point. Write a few sentences explaining how the quote you found relates to this chapter.

**Basic Facts About Wetlands**
mycorelibrary.com/wetland-ecosystems

# CHAPTER SIX

# THE FUTURE OF WETLANDS

The future of wetlands depends on how they are managed. One of the major threats to wetlands is pollution. Much of the pollution comes from farming runoff. This includes animal waste, pesticides, and fertilizers. Wetland plants can absorb some pollutants that flow through them, but they have a limit. People can help protect wetlands by reducing

Pollution can introduce chemicals that hurt wetland plants and animals.

Wetlands can continue to clean water after it has been treated at a wastewater treatment center.

the amount of fertilizers, herbicides, and pesticides in their yards.

Scientists are finding ways to use wetlands' cleaning abilities without hurting the ecosystem. One way is using wetlands for wastewater treatment. Wastewater is the dirty water that goes down sinks, tubs, and toilets. It is piped through sewers to wastewater treatment centers. Several processes at the centers clean the dirty water. When it leaves the treatment center, the cleaned water is called effluent. In some places, people use wetlands to further clean the effluent. This is called polishing. And it may help preserve wetlands in the future.

## Taking Action

Controlling invasive species is crucial to preventing wetland loss. In the Everglades, the National Park Service has removed approximately 2,000 Burmese pythons since 2002. Scientists believe there may be thousands more of these invasive snakes in the area. The invasive melaleuca tree is another threat to the Everglades. Several insect species that feed on melaleuca have been introduced to the area

## Wetland Water Recycling in Texas

The Tarrant Regional Water District provides water to 1.8 million people in and around Fort Worth, Texas. But a study projected that the population of the district would grow to 4.3 million by 2060. The district needed to plan how it would supply water to these people. One idea was to use the district's wastewater effluent. But effluent is not usually clean enough to drink. To solve this issue, the district built many acres of wetlands. The wetland plants clean the effluent. The clean water is then sent to the district's reservoir.

to prevent these trees from spreading. The melaleuca weevil, in particular, has been successful at damaging the trees.

The Ramsar Convention is an international wetlands protection program. The convention's mission is to conserve wetlands and ensure they are used wisely. Each of the 168 member nations has agreed to protect and manage at least one wetland deemed to be of international importance. There are nearly 2,200 of these wetland sites throughout the world.

As people continue to understand wetlands' value to the environment, they are taking more steps to protect them and return them to their natural condition. Many state, federal, and private organizations work to keep wetlands from being filled in or destroyed. They also help restore wetlands that have been damaged. By working together, we can regain and protect some of the wetlands that were lost in the past.

The following passage is from a United States Geological Survey report. It discusses changes in wetlands between 1900 and 1950:

> *Mechanized farm tractors had replaced horses and mules for farm labor during this half century. The tractors could be used more effectively than animals for drainage operations, and the old pasture land then became available for improvement and production of additional crops. In the Midwest and the North-central States, the use of tractors probably contributed to the loss of millions of acres of small wetlands and prairie potholes.*
>
> *In the 1930s, the U.S. Government, in essence, provided free engineering services to farmers to drain wetlands; and by the 1940s, the Government shared the cost of drainage projects.*

> Source: Thomas E. Dahl and Gregory J. Allord. "History of Wetlands in the Conterminous United States." USGS National Water Summary. US Geological Survey, 1995. Web. Accessed February 25, 2015.

## Point of View

This passage describes how using machines to farm affected wetlands between 1900 and 1950. Look back at the chapter. How has the perspective on wetland protection changed from the past. Do you think the change is good? Why or why not?

## The Pantanal

The Pantanal is one of the largest wetlands in the world. It lies in the center of South America, mostly in Brazil. The Pantanal covers 61,776 square miles (160,000 sq km). It is flooded annually from March through May. The Pantanal provides habitats for more than 650 bird species and 260 fish species. Some of the mammals found in the Pantanal are the giant river otter, jaguar, marsh deer, and tapir.

## Sundarbans

The Sundarbans is one of the largest mangrove forests in the world. It is located along coastal Bangladesh and India. The Sundarbans covers 3,861 square miles (10,000 sq km). The name *Sundarbans* means "beautiful forest." This wetland is home to the endangered Bengal tiger, as well as two endangered reptiles, the estuarine crocodile and the Indian python.

## Okavango Delta

The Okavango Delta is a seasonal wetland in Botswana. It is formed where the Okavango River meets the sands of the Kalahari Desert. The wetland is a network of channels, islands, and lagoons. Seasonal flooding occurs from August to September. It then serves as a watering hole for large mammals, such as elephants, lions, and hippopotamuses. More than 400 bird species depend on the Okavango Delta. Crocodiles also live here.

*The Sundarbans has one of the largest populations of Bengal tigers in the world.*

## Everglades

The Everglades stretch from central Florida south to the Florida Bay. Wetland plants range from saw grass to cypress and mangrove trees. The varied habitats of the Everglades make them home to many animals. Both the American alligator and crocodile are found in the Everglades. They are also home to the endangered manatee and Florida panther. More than 350 bird species live in Everglades National Park.

## Another View

Chapter Six discusses the future of wetlands. As you know, every source is different. Ask an adult, such as a librarian, to help you find another source about wetlands. Write a short essay comparing and contrasting the new source's point of view with that of this book's author. What is the point of view of each author? How are they similar and why? How are they different and why?

## Tell the Tale

Chapter Two of this book discusses the water cycle through wetlands. Write 200 words describing the journey a drop of water might take through a wetland. Describe the plants and animals the drop of water passes on its journey. Be sure to set the scene, develop a sequence of events, and offer a conclusion.

## Say What?

Studying wetlands can mean learning a great deal of new vocabulary. Find five words in this book you have never heard before. Use a dictionary to find out what they mean. Then write the meanings in your own words, and use each new word in a sentence.

## Surprise Me

Chapter Five discusses the functions of wetlands. Many of the benefits wetlands provide can be interesting and surprising. After reading this book, what two or three facts about wetland benefits did you find most surprising? Write a few sentences about each fact.

# GLOSSARY

**condensation**
the change of state from a gas to a liquid

**decomposer**
an organism that breaks down organic material, such as dead organisms

**effluent**
liquid waste or sewage

**endangered**
in danger of becoming extinct

**evaporation**
the change of state from a liquid to a gas

**food chain**
a series of organisms each dependent on the next as a source of food

**food web**
a network of overlapping food chains

**infiltration**
the movement of water from land into the soil

**photosynthesis**
a process in which producers use sunlight to create food

**producer**
an organism that uses solar energy or chemical energy to create the food it needs

**threatened species**
a species that may become endangered

**water cycle**
the constant movement of water from the atmosphere to the earth and back again

# LEARN MORE

## Books

Chambers, Catherine. *Threatened Wetlands.* New
   York: Crabtree Publishing, 2010.

Franklin, Yvonne. *Wetlands.* Westminster, CA:
   Teacher Created Materials, 2009.

Kaye, Cathryn B. *Make a Splash!: A Kid's Guide
   to Protecting Our Oceans, Lakes, Rivers &
   Wetlands.* Minneapolis: Free Spirit Pub. Inc.,
   2013.

## Websites

To learn more about Ecosystems of the World, visit
**booklinks.abdopublishing.com**. These links are
routinely monitored and updated to provide the most
current information available.

Visit **mycorelibrary.com** for free additional tools for
teachers and students.

# INDEX

# ABOUT THE AUTHOR

Nikole Brooks Bethea earned a bachelor's and a master's degree in environmental engineering and worked as a professional engineer for 15 years. Most of Bethea's publications are science and engineering books for children.